MY
MY

KRISTI MAXWELL

Saturnalia Books
105 Woodside Rd.
Ardmore, PA 19003
info@saturnaliabooks.com

ISBN: 978-1-947817-16-6 (print), 978-1-947817-17-3 (ebook)
Library of Congress Control Number: 2019952590

Cover and book design by Robin Vuchnich

Distributed by:
Independent Publishing Group
814 N. Franklin St.
Chicago, IL 60610
800-888-4741

Thank you to the editors of the following journals, where poems from this manuscript appear: *The Account*, *APARTMENT*, *Bennington Review*, *Black Warrior Review*, *Bone Bouquet*, *Boston Review*, *Dusie: the Tuesday Poem*, *Eoagh*, *jubilat*, *Masque & Spectacle*, *RHINO*, *Sprung Formal*, *Typo*, and *Transition: Poems in the Aftermath*.

I am grateful to the members of writing communities in Tucson, AZ; Knoxville, TN; Cincinnati, OH; and Louisville, KY, who have embraced my poems and me. I am especially grateful to the Tuesday night poetry crew: Jessica Farquhar, Ann DeVilbiss, Juan Ramirez, Michael Estes, and Kristen Miller—and to Karis Land. Thanks, too, to Brett Eugene Ralph and Ashley Taylor for building thriving community spaces in Louisville and for inviting me to share early drafts of these poems. I am grateful to the support I get from the University of Louisville English Department and especially from my Creative Writing Program colleagues, Kiki Petrosino, Ian Stansel, Paul Griner, and Sarah Strickley. Thanks, too, to all the students who've helped me think about my own poems by sharing their writing with me, and to Alex Niemi, for shifting from mentee to friend and reader. Deep thanks to Fran McDonald, for thinking with me, writing with me, and being around for the other things, too. I am ever grateful to Henry Israeli, Christopher Salerno, and the rest of the team at Saturnalia Books—thank you for continuing to support my writing.

Thank you to my family—the Maxwell family and the Sanders. And, of course, my love and gratitude to my favorite postscript, P.S., and our purr-bots, Gerty and Tang, who sat beside (and on) me during the writing of these poems.

for Perry Sanders,
for building with me a home
that's so friendly to acts of making
and
in memory of Arthur Smith—
"how little lasts, and how long"

CONTENTS

"These creatures are compound and nothing they do should surprise us. I don't mind, or I won't mind, where the verb 'to care' might multiply."

—Lyn Hejinian, *My Life*

SEA SONGS

1

on a day in which a sunrise embarrasses you
because of the way a cloud is handling the sun
an intimacy you yourself have missed
a light touch   a wisp or whiff of hand
you take a photograph, putting distance
between yourself and the scene

a wave breaks some news to the shore
it is nothing new   but still

a shell under a layer of sand, a swollen lymph node

when you were small, you thought everything you saw
was what you were going to see every time you looked

there are so many things to miss

a list goes here but the people around you
are going on about bacon and pork rind and the ear
of a pig   frozen blubber
the smoke points of various oils

you have commercial excess to thank
for the dry swimsuit   your second
that you will soon put on   a permissible exit

let go of your list   like a grudge you punish yourself with
thinking you are punishing another person

the sea grass looks like a great party from here
a crowd with arms   doing what arms do when
unconsciously mimicking sea grass caught up with wind

the tide of each eyelid covers the shore of each eye

there will soon be a man-o-war   showy as a fascinator
but with no head to hitch to or a great head, a remarkable head
but one one cannot imagine   so does not get to see

2

On screen the sunrise is an inverted exclamation point
part of a language   you don't speak

Uh oh if my bitmoji is my best self   my own sister
        a mythology   You can choose to be
sea-turtle attentive, caution tape and all

can choose cower or sea cow, herbivorous, buoyant, a cork
        a crock of *shhh*   a crack in   a Kraken

and when a bone breaks some loaf of skin   the bone shines
through   the bone a beam   what's suspect? sought?
        salt in the woo   a perfect season or seasoning

a seizing: as what the color blue has done to limit the sky
        as what the color blue has done to *lament*

                it is our approach that needs redoing
        the test-batch of our perception   thrown out
        the eye an icing on the dry cake of the mind

When you can't sleep at least there's a sunrise to trail
like a celebrity

                A tide scrolls up like a newsfeed
and you still hover over each shell, deciding if you like it
enough to note your liking, if you like it enough
to take

                    it might prefer you not like it, might prefer not
to leave

a wave debriefs the shore about the larger sea
            what has it to say?

There's a way to be tenderer but we've given tenderness away
to the language of meat

POEM STARTING WITH A MISREADING OF THE FIRST LINE IN "THE GLASS ESSAY"

I can hear little chicks inside my dream
They sound painted   they sound
like a feather's most profitable idea
They sound off   the sound is off
like something in the fridge   several days old
beans   in a different world, a newborn bean
cantaloupe   whatever it is that's our last stage
our vegetable matter   the world's last vegetable lamb
This is no Easter candy   not Chik'n or counterfeit beef
to have *a beef* with   a fist in the feast   A wooly aphid
parades like a cleaning pad over the rough face of a tree
What does the tree care   one must not only ask
but discover a method for asking   must harvest the fiber
to process the text   embroider the plant onto the sheet
along with initials   our love *so natural*
now   reminded of its seed   that the seed foresees
its own flower likely has nothing to do with the eye
it's shaped as   but who knows   what
knows   what

*

I can hear little hiccups inside my drain
The disposal needs to be addressed   *Dear disposal,*
dear waste   somewhere, the carcass of a deer
From the interstate, my love, driving, can find
and count every deer, coyote, fox   he animates
the field, brings the forest into focus *there,*
there   It's a wonder we say *the world*   a singular thing
a monocle resting on the galaxy's plump cheek
the other planets mere moles   no   I can hear
little hiccups inside my brain   everyone has their own
trick to make them stop   to resurface the esophageal road
There's been a hiccup   like an accident   bone exposed
metal plates stacked in the cupboard of one's body
not to be taken out   no matter the guest   We're asked
to think about what we have, to interrogate need
What's negated by terror   Here is one more torn interior
to tour   one more acorn of light to misplace
in the hillside   that swollen cheek   taunted by
each gauzy cloud that does nothing for it   ok it does
something   tossing out beads of ice   of rain
as if the earth had flashed something or at least
outstretched its arms, made hysterical by desire
like the rest of us   with no rest in us

*

I can earn little checks inside my dream   for my dream job
To knit a rind in which to enclose the wheel of sun
and its gooey light   To assign the barnacle to the shipwreck
To oversee the wound as it woos the throb   To edit the house's
biography of the last rooted tree   To tempt the glacial sadness
to carve   We are our own misinterpreted evidence
our own misdeal or mystic   our own bento box
into which the lunch of our being is divvied out among
the organic compartments   our limbs either rogue noodles or chopsticks
already snapped apart   ready to be used
regardless   or regard more   the zebras dressed up as tall grasses
a meter's ability to discern the worth of coins   the coin-fed
the corn-fed and the confession   the Mexican egg filled with confetti
despite having never been cracked   Was it that we wanted
to be amazed or a maze   Was it that we wanted to identify the husk
holding our succulent kernel   a core we can't give up
that punk   shielded by us   shielded from us
a two-way mirror   Where is the power: seeing oneself
or seeing another   That the mirror itself limits our conceptions
of empathy   suggesting as it does that we can deposit ourselves elsewhere
cash in, cash out   invest   The terms already decided
Do you agree to the terms

MANGROVE OR BRAMBLE

Rambling man-hole   the whole
mouth working   the lip a collar
signifying the worth of its work
I update my profile
relaunch the ship of my head
and head out
Lamb or wool of moonlight, loom
over us   who lack an edge
We do not judge the coastline's
monstrous face, but neither
do we take the earth in our hands
ask it   turn toward us
We growths that eventually
flatten, cease to show, we dogs
that don't place, despite
being barkless as a whittled branch
Whittle bitty, little birdie   whose throat
has been grafted with
an experiment we name song
but know is a peony
donning its burial gown
like a good melancholic
recoding the nature
of a bloom
O slender casket
slid into the mausoleum
of a vase
O petal, o peeve
Flashlight or flushlight
fishdark or to dart

because your body resembles
the game's implement
We ourselves game: ready or hunted
for jerky   or jerking off, jerking around
Shrug it off, sure   like a shore
eating up the placenta of foam
What are we meant to see as a child?
The dream contorts into a drain
Not even a leg here and a leg there
and a leg there and yet
we know what we're meant to see
so see, so *sí*   there is more
than one type of yes

From a Mouth in Which *Prayer* and *Error* Rhyme

What field aspires to be a lawn   a cow
a barrette in the field   holding up   an overgrown hill
            a canoe   a lake's barrette   but the water
is burn-slick   hairless   so the comparison will not do
no updo   no occasion

                a pewter hare is drilled to the wall
        the head of a hare   one imagines its body   behind
the wall   as if it there were a kink in materialization   the coordinates just
off
                a jacket off   a jacket rewriting the hare   a jackrabbit
when I try to imagine myself a rabid dog   I am nothing   more
than the patio of a bar in a college town   on foam night   whose suds

easily brush off   or dissolve   a novelty
        a set of flimsy dentures   making slack the morning's jowls
which is to say   whose desire is not a clumsy eater
the very concept of the crumb   keeps any of us   from truly finishing
        what we started   here we are then   undone

da da dum   somewhere   the mechanism   holding closed the wall
        holding back the boulder
                is tripped   this is the part
        where we run

You're the Only Audience I Ever Needed

At the wingspan chart   we extend our arms
and discover the bird   inside us—   are we egg
      or nest   damaged wing   eagle   egalitarian

a gal in a terrycloth robe   We change our clothes   our attire
      we change our attitude   our tire   our locks, hair-wise
and key-wise   our sheets   a survey asks   is "simple pleasure" an oxymoron

I bask in the freshly laundered linen   do I bask in them
or do I get under them and assemble   a passable joy
      in my emotional factory   overemployed—

The day is a slip-and-slide gone dry   no emoji
      matches the mood   one can barely move
but the heat is no hand   bearing down   no sweet claw
      in a baker's window   no wig of icing
glamming up   the crown of a cake

We blow a tire   we blow a shot   a nose   an ambiguous *it*
      the dream is a bridle   with which I'm able to steer my sleep

      the sun   a wheel   you can't reach to turn

      propped against a fence, a loaner bike   as planned
      and that   though it does not fit us   we ride
not even   paused by a plum rain   a plump drop
      a sandal   sacrificed to a makeshift   stream

PLENTY

To nanny ghosts   or just baby them
chill children, subtracted adults   I hold a ghost in the bassinet
of my mouth   a cherry tomato without a crown
Things I've learned: an AMBER alert is a bacronym,
created to honor the kidnapped and murdered girl
who inspired it   all-capped and angry   ghost in a letter
behind which is a hidden room   a whole word   a harnessed sound
the bacronym and acronym a kind of camping chair making cartable
the broader seat of a phrase   a kind of bacon
that's an ode to the pig   a fatty filmstrip preserving its narrative
Things I've learned   : if a drop of water hits you
while you're in a cave it's called a cave's kiss—what else when it hits you
is rewritten as a type of affection? plenty   you expected
a riddle but instead the bull of your expectation is ridden
the whole eight seconds   in the American tradition
we rid, we right   mistakes, high stakes we take stakes to the garden
and know the dirt has something to do with the harvest
and know the soil must be some part witch and martyr
all whom are returned to it   like a shirt that didn't quite fit
—for whose bodies   were we each made   beyond
our own   to be made and thus to lose the one you tailed
perhaps each of us is each docked   from the tail of god
and discarded   ostensibly to protect god
though   upon scrutiny   the practice is deemed
barbaric and mostly banned   it's too late for us
bloody wands   cast off   when the cast comes off
we know that signifies healing   the ghost of pain
griming up the plaster   our hallways webby, but repaired
Things I've learned: the webbing is mostly fat   the body
a tender spider   a double-yolked egg   plated,
photographed, circulated, devoured

Petal Texture

the text of petals
is pollen
in my history
ambiv(io)lence
and violets
and an iris detached
from an eye
give me sugar
before the surgery
but no food
your mouth figures
it out   like
a new pronunciation
we   the hardest
word   a hardestination
peat for a flower's repetition
turn *to earn* into *to get*
tug and fuck   a flock
as a bouquet of birds
rather than a banquet
what I don't want inside me
a stopped up sinus or a stop sign
the generosity of the bloom
interrupted   a soft reminder
our giving will not
be always wanted
what would you take back

AND THE DOLLARS, TOO

Among the irreconcilable things: the way pollution
amps up the beauty of a sunset   soupy neon
toxic pink   as if the sun were airbrushed onto the sky
        waiting to be eclipsed by a couple's ornate names
and the symbol for love   which the sun must regret
                        despite the magic of photosynthesis
        of any synthesis
is not itself   or that we might regret we've made
                        internal to ourselves
        Somewhere   a sleeve of cloud

            rolled up   to compensate for the heat—
        the A/C kicks on and kicks the curtain
from the pane   letting light   find its way in

and light sips from the flimsy lid   covering the cup of your eye
                it is not light   that is liquid here

in an ocean   a turtle is lured with indistinguishable meat
we distinguish as meat   because it bleeds   has blood
that loosens into a red jellyfish   and so   via metaphor
gets a second life   as a second animal   a second before
it's taken into the turtle's mouth   a guide's trick

to ensure   one sees what one's hoping to see
        because though one has paid   one has yet to tip
and the dollars too   have a metamorphosis   to fulfill

*

"I felt it shelter to speak to you."

—Emily Dickinson

After After

This was after we moved into pencil drawings of tree houses on stilts, but before the cows grazed in the diminishing field of the freckle signifying our face.

This was after a refusal of berries too close to rotting, but before self-consciousness about metaphor.

This was after the butter-soaked collard greens, but before we deflated the ache as if it were something reusable and easily stowed.

This was after the pimple you mistook for jam and, obviously, failed to wipe off, but before the last comma, which we obstinately misplaced.

This was after the bite mark, but before the tongue.

This was after the nosegay protecting the nose from the plague-stench, but before the video of the autopsy of the woman with a bra and panties matching your own.

This was after lushness, but before lushness.

This was after the ghosts caught fire and after their flimsy collage of light, but before the building conceived space and before the hard labor and before the dead men.

This was after the green shoe busted and the wool shoe, but before the description of a bus-struck owl.

This was after we knew, but long before saying.

AUBADE
for Megan Martin

Once stood in one's longest line

for another's brightest juice

from a vegetable's decimated body

made to make mates with one's buds

Once learned from a friend how to work

the mini stovetop espresso maker

and wondered what encounters YouTube

has destroyed: what one needs no longer

ask to be shown   a demo-

cratizing click   *You, too, can know*

Once slept in a living room with other living things

Once worried over the height of the space

at the base of an exterior door

What would come in and would it greet me

Even a grater could be interpreted

as greeting the block of cheese

but we know what happens there

but maybe a cheese's shredding is its experience

of the sublime   A dismantling

the disorientation that comes

A platform for departure from the station

of the self   A friend left behind but

turned back toward and acknowledged

by something in the face, nearly indetectable

as is a mutation in a gene long hunted

meant to prove something it doesn't

but seen now nonetheless

as it is

FESTIVAL SEASON

The surprise is how much isn't

Any longer

Scavenger hunt: find a betrayal

A ghost around 5 feet and alive

A ghoul in the gravy

A goil in a boi

The water's a tease

A woman questions a star

This is no interview

But night's interrogation

The dream as one interrogation tactic

Who is "the company" – commercial or intimate

Commercialized intimacy

I would rather not see you than look for you

The noise just another version of silence

I weep for what's forgotten of the unforgettable

My tear is the un–

Scavenger hunt: the leg of a flower, the cowboy who is a cool question, the lips in a rose, a breeze that robs the thief of heat

Would one rather be impressionable or unimpressed

To take in the world

That abundant stray

ON SEEING

a tattoo of a

magnifying glass magnifying

an eye

miniature of a fox

eye pinned

to the slipper

of a foxglove

OF THE TECHNOLOGIES

To prove I am no robot, I tap bridges, I tap street signs, I tap "that ass," which is to say, I am colloquial, a colonist making do in a new colony of language, a weather making dew on a flower's polished nail. My gratitude is plagiarized by each fruit's stone, by milk in a white bowl, tongue on my tongue. In my basket, a virtual bouquet of paper flowers I decide not to buy, wanting wilt, wanting ceremony, the rapture of a stem, the cyst of a bud that ruptures into bloom.

A WHOLE GLOBE

I hit the wrong heart
Three times
I flew the wrong paper plane
The word was waste
The work, too
Because disposable
Packaged to be so
Which existence
Should we sample
This time
Which brand
Without forgetting
To cancel
Before we're charged
O bull of commerce
O Capital Bully
O fashionless comma
Not an earring after all
Though you sit in my lobe
I hear you
In the pause
I make a whole globe of you
And move myself
A mountaintop
More vulnerable than
Than an excessive word
In an editorial eye
It wasn't my imagination
It wasn't yours
And yet

And yet
Before a yeti was a product
In stores
It was a product
Of the mind
A myth
Or possibly miffed
By the mythologizing impulse
Through which we undo and
Remake the world

In Memory of the Sound of a Silent Letter

You have your Zen moment
I'll have my brazen one
A ghost's ghost is its 'h'
Teaching me
To be my own ghost
Teaching you
It is our own death
That haunts us
Do *haunt* and *hunt* share
The same root
Or just the same feeling?
Does grass ever tire
Of being armed
With its blade or of metaphor
Which armed it—
It could have been legs
Of grass
Doing a synchronized
Swim routine
In the pool of earth
Into which it dove

Red Song

My own lack of trust
My own lack
My own slack I don't cut myself
though I cut myself
on a misplaced mandolin
How oh ow
How oh ouch
The blood comes like a soundtrack
consistent though light at first
then foreground rather than background
then on the cabinets and floor

THE FOAL WAS ALREADY THERE
for Fran McDonald

You bring the colt to the hot tub
in the stall of your voice, it having been
stalled from emerging into your thoughts
when earlier a friend asked the name
of a baby horse not wanting a particular name
Juju, Ginger, Esmerelda, etc. You watch
the colt dip into the water's surface.
The jets, on a timer, go off, as if
they could meander—a new animal
making some sense of the world.

DRIP DRIP

My canoe tongue
won't capsize
in the lake of
my thought.
The water remains
uncrimped—
like midcentury
hair. Let's get this
straight: metaphor
is not conversion,
and a steak is both
cow and ache.
The stomach almost
holds ache.
But for that bustle of *e*.
Egress, egret, ease.
The stomach
mostly holds ache.
Shapely crypt.
This was before lack
was a brand of hunger.
This was before ice
was water's pelt
and the body was
skinned.

MICHIGAN

What fool am I?
Whose foil?
With a tin ear
I hear the flower's
flatline winter
has resuscitated.
On cue I was
rescued. Uncool
I was destroyed.
My own ravaged
Troy I horsed
around with.
Suspended within
a school of
frozen fish.
Whose map may I
Michigan? Whose
mission may I
give a saintly name
and thwart? War
is no fever so
does not leave.
We reckon with
its rawness,
clean up like
children unused
to chores.

SPRING OFFSPRING

Minor sons
Of little note
Or young
Miner sun
Digging into earth
And coming
Up with gold
Like a swimmer
Coming up
With breath
As if it were
An idea water
Shared with
The body
The body then
Felt inclined
To circulate

JAG

For this to be soft as a tear
and as ephemeral—
though the swollen eyelids
betray the jag
that itself recalls
a jaguar and now the tear
is a strong animal, glistening
as it tears through your field
and you don't know if that tall grass
is anger or sadness or frustration
because you are hungry
though you have forgotten
what exactly is your prey
you have a phone for that
so enter your terms and search
and choose relevance as that which
determines order

On Working It Out

The bicep has two heads, but, unlike Janus, no faces

We work to make each head discernable

Inflect or flex

An exercise in tone

True or false: because I'm being figurative,

I need not be accurate

If the body were to have a register, where would its cash be stored?

A value question

What to make the body cha-ching,

what to make the body count?

I know the best edit I've ever made

How my days opened up

like a lush, cooing into an ear-shaped rim

Doubling

to lean when

told to lean

then to lean

without lean

being voiced

having learned

the cues from

your other body

GO FIGURE

Once tried on your friend's pants

in a rented bathroom in secret

as if this might tell you

a secret about your own body

Once became conscious

of the discharge in your own jeans

should your friend be tempted

then seduced—putting her body

where yours belongs

(Once chose not to use the word

secretion   though you

even without secret's echo

liked to imagine parenthesis

the labia of punctuation)

(what, then, are words)

OFFHAND HANDS OFF

May as well be the incapable understudy of clouds. We all bring our shapes to the sky.
Train car from which departs two caped men. A volcano coddled by fog. A mass of tissue
it's imperative to remove. We transfer the game to beer foam and drink in the pistol the
panicked rose becomes. We give our middle finger to comparison, diminisher of is
though is is the bridge connecting tooth to cliffside encased in the snow globe's mouth.
Gah. Is as it turns out is a petri dish, is the entrée in the dish itself, resting like a steak
that will sound out its last bloody word in a second. Hold on. Just a second. I'm renaming
this ache melt so I can understand the body as affirmation, a mountain more traversable
than not. One second. Hold up. My newsfeed is again today a study in the failure to see.
It used to be I thought of the classroom when I thought of hands raised.

Hello, detective

Rename me the quiet execution of a nail
Rename me mouthwork and guesswork
Gethsemane, a Sunday in France
Rename me no widow
Rename me no whited-out error
or whittled branch, no wood debris
No bereavement
Rename me concussion, cocoon, ca-caw,
a series of useless birdsong, bird-sound,
the brain's own birth-pain, delivering a thought
Rename me coddler or god
witness or withness
an unforgiveable act, an ax or an ask
Rename me afraid
but do not name me without
Do not name me without
not minnow
Do not name me bait or beaten or deterred
Rename me turd, but not porcelain, not flesh
Rename me commotion
Rename me the proximity of salt and sugar
as the distance between assault and assure
Rename me sugar-assured, rename me
ushered, rename me hush
do not rename me hush
do not take us out of the world
Rename me a series of pills
but not swallow
but not even a swallow's wingspan
or prey

Rename me prayer or drawer into which
one folds her desperation
but do not name me opened
and do not open me
Rename me father, further, pelt,
trade, treason, logic, and lube
Rename me bunny-tail of moon on the wide ass of night
Rename me after accumulation, after the fact
Rename me after after
Rename me then
Rename me any, rename me anon, avast,
a Kevlar vest never needed
Rename me sinew
Rename me insinuation
Rename me remain but not remains
Do not rename me tooth-sized or canine
blasted or blessed
Rename me have, rename me as having
Rename me sleep, but not sleeper, sleep

*

"There are always more leaves than flowers. In the breeze they occupy the eyes with the wobble of the rough circles of a self. I, with crashing consequity, waited, wanting to have experienced many, many things."

—Lyn Hejinian, *My Life*

IRL

I'm sorry   I hope you get the pleasure
To be sorry to hope   To be sorry for
pleasure   a tube of sorrow-cream squeezed dry
          my main squeeze a feather fallen
from the lovebird's wing   into the road and
picked up   like an accent   To use the pillow
of one's voice   to throw
          like a ventriloquist   onto the couch of one's thought
thus   "bringing the room together" like those
of different minds   coming to an unlikely consensus
coming to   after passing out   how the sound comes
into focus   the brain's radio dial turned slowly up
          but whose fingers   do the turning
          whose ears hear the erring   holding court
courtship's held hand   handheld   divisiveness
One conjures a god   who can handle the blame
          who can be a lake   when swimming's in order
who can be the hand's heel   when the vending machine of one's self
                              needs a good thwack
          who can be a fork   which itself conjures food
who can be an ellipses   allowing an abbreviated passage
                    to pass as the whole

Or the Light is a Creak in the Cloud's Sound-scape / a Creek in the Cloud's Landscape

She said   the lantern is cranky   with light   or
        daylight makes   the lantern mean less   whereas night makes it
mean   and less mean   Work for the light   You have to
crank the lantern   to break through its stone-cold face   so the light
        smiles through   a crack of light in the broken plate the day is
                each morning I pull the wool
blanket   over my head   I pull the dark cherry's meat
        from a stone
                How do we discern which terror
papers the interior's walls   which cut-out best captures
trauma's shape   now project it   cut the flower's stem
        an iris with a drooping beard
        One sits behind a sheet   and behind him   one shines
a flashlight   a shadow begins to talk   and then another
        a rock sings   or water sings the rock   or a stone
is the tongue in the stream's mouth   weighing down its song
        our own tongues   streams   feeding into each other
        or streamers   floor-bound too soon   and yet
something rises   in us   a false sun   falsetto sun
        a voice going dark   a pit restored in a pitiless place

ONGOING EFFORTS

Memory is a foam   frothing the lip
     of the brain?

I wake floating and blind and hear my love beside me
listening to a live feed
of the police chief talking about ongoing efforts to locate the body
of a swimmer   by now surely drowned

     to recover   the body
of one who was swimming
who is no longer
a swimmer   who is
no longer

I wake floating   stretching my eyes
     attempting to reach an image   all around me blackened

To exist in a smudge

     I make out my own dissolving hand
a hand-me-down image   retained from last night's screening
of *Back to the Future*

     when I finally break through   the hymen of sleep
     there is no blood
     but neither is there a noun with fidelity
     to me and
     me alone

each of us   an x among x's   seeking brackets
     awaiting substitution
     and its prerequisite
     erasure

Violin

I was mere lint caught in the threading of the pocket
of unhappiness   Which is to say, I couldn't be pulled out
of it
          No clarity in the wood, no hidden
or future violin   Though I am the bed's voice
you are its vocabulary   The lamp of speech
A lantern swinging the dark's kid-body
          higher, higher, faster, faster—
In the dining room I hear   cat food hit the plate
At least this part of the day   is "taken care of"—a minute
                    offed as if it were a man
                    we can't have back

Weren't None of Us

How was she? She was burnt out. You mean she was a thing flame had gone through. She was a thing flame had gone through. She was through? Thrown. Such a queen of sadness. No queen of a thing. But orderly. An orderly of sadness. Not such keen sense as that. She was a tree on which lay scented-ness. Licentiousness. But did it mean? It did mean.

Plank of muscle

quiver walks

out on

She took a quill to quiver and paid my name to it, paid in letter
from leather sack, sacked a letter from a lesser word.

The object is not lost but it feels lost.
The object is not lost but it feels loss.
The object is not lost but I feel lost.
The object is not lost but I am a host to loss.

A hostage of it.

What a smooth invention is leaving.

We snatched the bone from the thought.

O Fido me home. O fight for me home.

She was a purring thing. A breakfast habit. A hell-bent. An earth-tweaked. A little beast
some weeks became, and rusted now the tongs of our bodies
                              refusing to pick each other up. That ante
we owed to the muscle-bawdy whew. To the not-quite through though through.
The never-never plundered, and the laundry done. The den of done stuff
                              done made new. Dung makes new
as its fertile-lazing self. Our own manure-selves,
coaxed toward growth.

In the Middle of Something

As far as structure goes, he's the matching edge
to my French cleat, my built-in   As far as consumption goes,
he's my last fever or purchase   my return

As far as   far out   a farce and pout
a force and a pow   which is to say another gunfire

          pop pop   Papa   da-
ng

We sit on the porch and debate firework or bullet
We go to the message board where others debate
We do not chime in   being no instrument
          being not   man-handled by wind or whim
We drive through the neighborhood and keep an eye out
for teddy bears and fabric flowers strapped to chain-link
          To commemorate   Come, Memory

Come, Mammary   For the body to take care of its own needs
          to take care of one's own   to take
          drink of my milk, drink of my milklessness   in this lack-station

As far as night goes, he's a tusk of moon   sawed off
As far as pears go, he's poached   Bosc man   order us
order up   at least your hunger takes you places
at least your hunger was a good enough mentor to ambition
at least you could make the decision to fast   having food
          to refuse

Poem Whose Composition Leads to the Term *Winterkill*

Inside a ponderable spring
(a pond-durable spring)

but is this water or season
is there a cod
or are there petals in the shape
of them swimming toward the hellish bait
bobbing in and out of clouds (it's the cloud
that moves
lifted as a fin on a fish that floats
in decomposition (unwritten))

(a dead sail) (unlike the parenthesis
prepared for wind))))) though boat-less (are our
words not something we set between
the shores of our mouths))

where did we once search
for stars
that wasn't the sky
or a boulevard in Southern California
or a bistro nestled in a borough
of New York

there was a trick to finding a belt
a certain cinching of the eyes
a point of reference
a fresh hole   you dig
like a '70s protagonist

the ghost in your face already treating
your cheeks like beach towels
laid out for it

(wan tan ting wan tan ting wan ting ting
ting wanting tan wanting wan sun in waiting
wanting wanting
an ant of wanting carting the corpse
of the storm to the rose

every rose has its storm
an origin story
a sustainable orgy)

in a century in which
even our beds are queens

and we do lie prostrate
though not before them

though we do submit
a bi-syllabic self
to split (the knife a hyphen
suturing the fruit
or seeming to
in the still image
of the scene)

there is a future already
quarreling with coral
a grief-reef, a reef-grief

yet nothing
is froufrou about a tear
except its surrealist representation

a jewel sewn on to a face

an oblique lesson about
loss's value

In a Pickle

I wish not to reserve the gherkin
for the king her king, especially

The ferns leaked green

There were threats of jail-time
There were threats of Jell-O shots, too
One came to fruition one bore fruit
One blurred fruit and hoof Huff on

We came to from the coma of our apathy
We clamored for a path like a sandpiper
a meat-studded shell

A truth inhabited the shell of a fact
before it was hollowed out
by that which found its own value
greater What shall we eat

I cannot un-see *die* in *dine*—
the headstone an *n* becomes
The missing epitaph

My own tongue a flattened headstone
Who toppled it pink empire

punk empire if only one were ruled
by the tenant of one's own mouth

Hold your tongue sweet infant
You are no sad birthday cake

There are still more women inside you

*

"Are we stowaways?"

—Rae Armantrout

(Pre)Occupation

There was a moment I wanted to remember.
A specific irritation. An impenetrable rind
of an orange. A kind of eyelash in the eye
and the eye is our love
and our love is our saturation.
An archaic Polaroid waved dry. I may commit more
unnecessary acts than necessary.
I may lend my support to a faulty reading.
The window in the pregnancy test
of the mind only dimly responsive
so we make a guess rather than a baby.
A magic stick. A matchstick. A lipstick. A dipshit.
I live in a house that is not my house
surrounded by things that are not my things
though aesthetically they could be
in the sense I would pick them out
and several of them could afford.
The camel saddle has been googled.
The delphinium-blue dishes from France.
A disposable cup not disposed of.
Being adorable is a fine if ephemeral protection,
little goat. My day is made of money
because I am preoccupied by debt.
The purchase of a mood. An unpacking.
The fear a parent will die and the fear a parent will soothe.
The fear I owe an apology I withheld
and that apology was
the soothing water and I have bracketed
a life that was not mine to punctuate
much less close. The fear my hand will be hung in a fence

I touch from the window of a moving car
and detached from the larger part
of my body like a vacuum attachment
one cannot reach a certain crevice without.
My husband is new. A benevolent virus.
There are bodies on the shower curtain,
I remind myself, so I don't get confused and mistake them
for bodies outside the shower itself. Pulling the curtain back,
I crimp the bodies. I close my eyes and accordion fold
my desires into a manageable fan and cool myself.
There is no space in the recycling bin. There is
no space in the garbage. What's to be done?
To be simultaneously empty and full.
To be *put out* or *to put out*. Turning our girls
into trash with our language. Upsets today
upset tomorrow. O, vacillation. O, metaphorical vaccine.
The 'o' is a prick but is this fairytale or slang.

Accountability

A tarot card wears a gown, which is to say, a gown
is printed on it. The sleeve of the gown bends
in an embodied way though the only body is blue
background, cradling an unfashionable cloud.
And though I do not read Tarot, the card comes out
of my own deck, an Emily Dickinson artist pack
from which it separated itself during a recent move
and came to be propped on the nightstand,
though, only today, six weeks after arriving,
do I look up its meaning (see "The Hermit," see
her mitt reaching into the oven of her thought—
see also the information page for the new teal
robe on its way to me and which I will wear
to prepare coffee to take to the porch
on which I will, good hermit, introspect,
reconnoitering the rim for specter or scepter,
for a kingly speech to overthrow). In my new home,
fleurs-de-lis appear like conspicuous Waldos,
the city named after King Louis XVI, thus
making it, according to the Unofficial Louisville
Fan Site, "one of the few cities in the world
named for an executed criminal" (I'll be heading
to a different source soon, away from the season
of sore sons, revolution reduced to a commemorative
red string, thin and pinned tight enough to the neck
to pass as blood rushing to a life's closing sale
where, yes, all inventory must go, though it is not
prices that are slashed). After Katrina,
enough New Orleans residents tattooed a *fleur-de-lis*
on their wrists to call it a trend, city annexing

the suburb of a body in which the soul for once
is not priced out. The dualism is outdated
and the binary false, but our fictions are real, in terms
of their effects, which one gathers and turns
into a platform for solidarity. The fake mayonnaise
on my plate has turned into a miniature of a transparent
mountain unexplored by my hunger and now
doomed to encounter an impossible storm—
is it metaphors that are corrupted by the world
or metaphors that corrupt? I hold my tongue
like a seat someone is coming back for,
but another takes it, and I don't protest, because,
ultimately, the practice of saving seats annoys me,
and what one claims, one may be forced to keep.
I intuit myself a clumsy shepherd, an inauthentic crab
with a meddling softness, a statue on loan to the state.

NIGHT WITH DILL, LEMON

By my mattress topper on a borrowed mattress
in a rented frame, a night stand and *Stand*,
the American Civil Liberties Union
magazine, also not mine
though made mine by mine eyes'
word habits, each word a habit they put on
like good nuns or, at the very least, recognizable

ones. A cutting from a Christmas cactus from my
grandmother's yard in Florida where I
have not returned since a rented yellow convert-
ible Mustang carted me
from airport to dirt road
for her funeral in a year two airlines
still supplied grievance flight prices to those who could prove their

grief with doctor's call or obituary thrives
on a yellow table, also not mine,
with hearts cut into the sides of it and a paint
job that suggests craft project
over boutique purchase
and that someone "poured their heart into it" like
a cold tea brought into the yard in a glass where a tarp

would have been laid to protect the grass from the ex-
cesses of art. My sister, who, when
visiting, once watered the cactus and wrote a
note in its voice urging more
attention and thus bet-
ter care, would be glad to see it, perky as
a pom-pom. Rah-rah. Given my 21st century

marriage, you will not be surprised to learn my hus-
band and I do not own each other
either, though we owe each other a great deal, a
fact we celebrated last
night with dill, lemon,
garlic, salt, and oil dressing a fish dressed in
an aluminum onesie that kept it warm after ex-

iting the oven's womb into which we together
had inserted it like a type of
euphemistic seed. We are not the first to eat
our young. Still, I am more meat-
less than heartless, the food
I prefer to eat having never had a
heart, with the exception of artichoke and romaine, which

remained last night in the crisper, which is to say
I am among those with choices and new-
ly less in debt, having received my first tenure-
track paycheck and having paid
off two of three credit
cards and having selected a restaurant
to try for brunch and having made a list to aid me in

the grocery store a five-minute walk from "my" house.
I see already how all this having
could lead to hating, self-directed or project-
ed onto me and so I
lift the *tv* out from

inside *hating* and *having* and turn it on
to distract myself while I finish a poem as if it

were a nightcap meant to appease the infant
anxiety determined to spoil the
milk of sleep.

MY FINGERNAILS ARE NEW TO ME

I celebrate the removal of matter
from between my teeth. The internet ad-
monishes: explore the hidden wounds
of national parks! Exclamation point
as geyser: blow. Line of blow. Annoying things:
napkin holders overstuffed with napkins
so that pulling one means pulling all.
Now for the scene in which your bowel
movement is a parasite's #humblebrag.
I do not believe there are two kinds
of people though I hope for kindness
in people. The ravens' opposite.
Morning for my cats is learning the difference
between cicadas, katydids, and locusts. My first
stepmother's friend, a Katydid, as I suspect
many Katies become, injected within
the stem of her own name and reborn there.
My morning is a plant's underside
the color of dried blood whose life is
entrusted to me and suddenly I am
the darkened stoop of a safe haven
where a basket filled with a creamy-faced
baby is dropped. Explore the hidden wounds.
The unnatural park of consciousness.
The hacked-down growth. A lime tree
in a lemon-colored pot. The poem
is a test kitchen where the donut metaphor
fails. I am sorry, baby. Maybe next time.

It's Either Maintain or Destroy

He finds his bike's doppleganger on a side street
in China, on a telephone pole in the West.
We train ourselves to see similarities,
and yet someone would sing the Meyer lemon
amongst regular lemons to texturize the song.
The make-up artist has but one mandate:
simulate each bruise so each pain is recognizable.
I'm treating my body like there's something inside it
as a way to care for my body, to misguidedly build a wall
between desire and flesh, to split the infinitive like a hair
or a family. I might as well invite Sylvia Plath's daddy.
I might as well cancel the subscription to our deaths.
He finds my crying in a bar and renames me.
I try to French fry the sad away. I try to Rummy it.
A friend is posting a series of Rumi memes.
There I go, dating this poem, though
it will not pay for a thing. Maybe each poem
is always already a plea for accountability,
asking something from language.
Lately, when I see *banking on language to mean*,
I also see *banking on language to be mean*.
And the idea of banks brings the idea of withdrawal.
But your drawl brings love to me, in the cooler
of your voice, with space enough to hold me,
an organ ready for exchange.

A Pause

Sleep's hoverboard is bogged down
by waking. What I want to say is I was hovering
over my sleep like a rainforest's immaculate sweat,
a cataract that turns the air into the laid-out ghost
of every pianos' white keys—a bygone music.
I am no surrogate for an orphaned gorilla.
The gorilla suit no longer on loan.
Summer's tragedy is fall's trend then the landscape's death-
mask we laud as wintry, as pause's win. A pause when?
My hands are no longer together—divorced from clapping,
but show me anyway what you can do: unhitch
the celebration from the act. The celebrity
from the flash. Maybe we are all fish sticks mistaking
the sea-colored plate as a kindness.

On Toxicity

What is the work

I have not been doing

      I work to ID the unholy rhinoceros
and compose a list of things I never expected
to find in my home: brass knuckles,
a Glock, three copies of Glück's *Wild Iris*,
a sausage party. Okay, so I expected
the latter, but only one in which there is
a critical evaluation of the limits of
sex and meat. A meatlessness. A placeholder
for pork's ennui. My own holes are hosts
to the instruments of devastation. Each body always
already the antithesis of a "safe space."
Are you a tough or tender meat? We
unruly harbors. We aviaries void of birds.
We knifeless sheaths. Pick up the bloodless trope:
has there been a letting, or was emptiness
the starting place?

BLANKS

We like our men bad. We like our women dead.
We like our _____ _____. We like our _____ _____.
We like our erasures like we like our bets: unlikely or profitable.
We like our best bets horse-free. We like our whore's bath
idiomatic so we can keep sex work unhygienic.
We like our blank unfilled, but fillable. We prefer our jugs
sonic over buoyant, lest we feminize the honky tonk,
who plays, who applauds. We prefer to kid over having them.
We prefer to embarrass like butter subjected to heat
rather than to approximate a baffled sunset, horizon-less.

ELEGY FOR THREATENED WORDS

It wasn't that the cake was vulnerable
to teeth so much as meant for eating—a mouth's entitlement,
or, in indulgence's own belly, a Lego project of cells, a fetus.
That the baker was transgender
had nothing to do with his refusal to bake reveal-cakes, science-based,
announcing *it's a girl*/*I'm a boy*—rather, a commitment to a diversity

of goods and to the good of diversity.
There are plenty of other things to let take on *vulnerable*:
all that is subject to wilting, a fan's ear drums, evidence-based
studies, a ruler's belief that praise is an entitlement,
slugs, a centenarian's epidermis, the very notion of transgender
if we stop asking "what sex is the baby?" of each viable fetus.

Not to feed us is not to defeat us.
Even the Ark foregrounds diversity,
even the market saturated with goods, be they for trans
and/or cis consumers, a sister or a different sibling, catalog-vulnerable,
the very glint in the eye of capitalism, a title meant
to mean something, but based

in the wrong analogy, an algae dirtying the tank of logic, evidence-based
and reasoned. Sometimes, it's all too much, and I curl like a fetus
inside the tub's performance of an amniotic sac, self-care an entitlement.
I search on the Internet for the best diver city
and pack my wetsuit and rent some oxygen, my lungs vulnerable
to collapsing. "Every vacation is self-care!" my gender-

queer travel agent insists, knowing there are certain places where my gender
expression makes me more welcome than them, based
on another's comfort, whether that person feels vulnerable
about his or her own flimsiness, the custard of every identity, from fetus
to agèd aviary, aflap with one's own contained diversity.
"Self" is the entitlement

upon which all other entitlements
rest. "Self" is a pool in which all identities swim: fit and transgender,
preferrer of backstroke, preferrer of breast, farrier, ferryman, Head of Diversity
and Inclusion, bottom, top, one who values science-based
research, one who thinks science is bunk, top bunker, bottom bunker, fee-tussler,
arguing for fewer or more, lower or higher, fighting for the vulnerable

or against the vulnerable, protecting or retracting entitlements,
allowing the fetus of fact to grow into legible news, a trans-
lation based not on Autocorrect or autocracy—not divestment in place of diversity.

Rose Garland Cento

Why is it no one ever sent me yet
roses that sing the heavy steps of the ploughman?
Had I not been awake, when a child then whispered
the only tattoo I want this year is
the sponge, not oceans, or stars, wronging your image
like letters—pages spread and curled, bloomed like
time you have wasted for your rose. Rejoice:
he who dares not grasp the thorn should never
outlive the rose that grew from concrete when
the language of roses shifted under our feet.
We complain better than any cabbage.
Rose, oh pure contradiction, joy of being
No time. Grieve for roses when the forests
are burning. O Rose thou art sick. It seems strange
an idealist notices that a rose smells.
I had roses, and apologized to no one.

THE BOAT WAS A THOUGHT THE RIVER WAS HAVING

Words I have evacuated from my mouth: ginger, chokehold, June
      To decipher, to "make out"—to hold
the body to language
like a slide to light
The erotics of seeing
or the rotted image pruned from the mind
thus "nipping the bud"   the work (worth)
of repression
      In a different life the patio holds
our conversation about the dead child
The beer a bassinet in which we rock
Stray hair stray bullet stray cat
Unsturdy—a day in which
one feels herself an understudy
in her own life
      It was the photo of you
using ginger root as antlers
or the shyness with which we spoke
in a line for a familiar bathroom—
to be the precipice knowing looks over
before backing away
I want to hold this memory down
by the neck
      We remain uneven
A plot in a genre that doesn't prioritize plot

On Unnatural Nature

The creek draws a profile
on the valley. What they once called
a weak chin, as if it were responsible for
and had failed the weight of
the head it punctuates. The rear of a period
anchoring an exclamatory tail. An inkwell
in which rests a quill, aslant. A pen *its* inkwell.
An inkwell *its* pen. A distinction
sexual penetration has made matter.
The language of possession.
The phallic nature of a vertical line.
A hill looks over the creek.
An act of condescension or care.
The hill is an exercise in browns.
Is death's easel.
My language a poor apprentice.
The creek is not a wound
despite metaphor. There is a face
though, in repose. A face larger
than your own. A face with
infinite tongue. The creek is not
entrails, though its earth may in fact be
racked, stretched, nearly quartered,
made ecstatic with its own rending
without a choice of its own.

ON THE COMMON SUFFIXES OF TOWNS

Near the pit, beneath a sturdy toupee of wood,
a rabbit face fleeces the yard, a soft iceberg
loosening in the heat, emerging as a mere
animal body, a mirror supporting a ton
of dandelions, were this a still from vaudeville.
We name the decapitated mountain Dale,

inspired by the valley-girl comedies of our youth, the dales
in which the deals of our innocence would
have been brokered, had we bought into the concept of evil.
As if one's foundational terms are grey burgers
to be picked up from life's congested drive-thru, a tongue
praised for unearthing a bun's repressed oration, a mere

smear of dogma any adequate napkin could undo. *Mere*
can be enough, lodged like a splinter, in the dale-
imitative sole of vulnerability's foot, with the allegiance "a ton"
has to hyperbole. At a time we had not yet met the wood
anniversary, in a time in which the Earth's favored icebergs
seemed incapable of occupying the verb "to melt," a ville

took on age, like a child, thrilled, knowing not of any evil
concocted by progress. As if the world were no more than a mare,
giving birth to things. Here, imagine humanity burgles
"the world" of its definition. Here, know the indel-
ible believed wholly in its ability to endure. Why would
it not, used so assuredly in poems? By now, the automaton

can rewrite our canon. By now, our waste exceeds a ton
as a useful measurement. The brain prepares the villa
of a young summer to be entered—the olive wood,
unoiled all these years, to be grasped. What seemed mere
instead a habitable memory, a place to move, a dale
among he'll's—*he will, he will.* He won't. You didn't. A *brrr*

seasoned each sigh. Winter learned what summer knew. Burr-
adorned, nature mentored bedazzlement. Still, a mitten
of leaf, failure-bound, bound to fall, got lost by an idle
branch. Had we taught it of flight, of Wilbur and Orville,
of broad siblinghood, had we not confused the sea with *la mère.*
Un-warrant the new design. Build a tree out of this wood.

BEFORE AFTER

The bread-king appeared
in breaking's misspelling: his rise
accidental, and, now, yeas exchanged
for yeast.

The laughability tempers
the tragedy, but does not change it.
Language always the jester.

What do you think the Cheshire cat's
grin was made of if not the word teeth?

But it wasn't the word, though t's
touched t's to demarcate each tooth
in the cartoon mouth. It was the idea—

and the irreconcilability between the idea
and its articulation.

HOUDINI

My name is pregnant
with small I's. Like everyone
else, I am given a shoulder
of self to shrug and a mouth
of self with which to salivate.
We were fooled into thinking
the moon had a name,
mistaking glint for identity,
mistaking clouds for an eraser's smudge
betraying language.
Our bank account fails us
because it refuses to buff up.
It grows weaker. It un-grows.
O, atrophy. An un-trophy.
My beloved punctuation
forms the back slash
that breaks the line of my sleep.
I name the moon Houdini
in order to treat the day
as its magic.

Without without

In an inbox, bumblebees are dying
like lights in a light-soaked room in the midst
of an energy drought, power out
any moment, even the sun, a pimple on course
to be drained—so the light rightly praised,
the light "bathed in" by those of us
committed to verbs, committed
to absence's recovery, the light still a thing
"working for us," golden light, especially,
 turmeric-light, pollen-aping—essentially,
honey's rumored performance of light.
For the bumblebees to be dying
like this conjured light, the light must agree
to forfeit its own renaming: no darkness,
no needle sewing shut and silencing
the stony lips encircling a flaming tongue,
no flicker. No sole fucker to accuse.
To delete the bumblebees
from the inbox does not destroy
the bumblebees but nonetheless you feel compelled
to keep them, reluctant to engage the meaning
of this ineffective preservation. Your allegiance
to technologies that have not served the bees,
that may well not serve you,
that may well corrode. The hive mind
no suitable asylum. The bees will not be last.

"Poem Starting with a Misreading of the First Line in 'The Glass Essay'" | Anne Carson's poem begins with the line, "I can hear little clicks inside my dream." "Acorn of light" is borrowed from Pound's Canto CXVI.

"You're the Only Audience I Ever Needed" | The title for this poem comes from Rian Johnson's heist film, *The Brothers Bloom.*

"Hello, Detective" | This poem was first published in *The Account,* alongside the following "account" of the poem: In the spread of a week, I was in the ER because of acute pain caused by a herniated disc, and my husband was in the ER after being beaten and robbed while biking home from work. My mind was on the tenuous, my mind was on the body—that spectrum of fragility and resilience. I'm sure most of us have experienced frustration at our inability to help someone in the way we'd like—the texture of my mornings changed; my day began with a call to the detective because a call made me feel like I was doing something. I got married somewhat spontaneously in July 2016, and, to my surprise, I liked my new name: wife. I wanted to keep it. This poem is as much about the talk I did not have with the detective as the talks I did. It's about the collision between grief and celebration. It's either lullaby or tornado or spell. It's a poem on holding, a poem on hold, waiting less patiently than it might.

"Night with Dill, Lemon" | This syllabic poem was written in response to rereading Robyn Schiff's work with my students in ENGL 504 in Fall 2016.

"Elegy for Threatened Words" | This sestina was written in response to reports that the CDC was being pressured to exclude certain words from its budgetary requests: transgender, diversity, science-based, evidence-based, vulnerable, fetus, and entitlement.

"Rose Garland Cento" | This poem was composed in celebration of the first Poetry Derby at the Kentucky Derby Museum at Churchill Downs. It lines are harvested from lines about roses in Rainer Maria Rilke, Ana Castillo, William Blake, Stephen King, Antoine St. Exupery, Juliusz Slowacki, Helen Humphreys, H.L. Mencken, John Daniel Thieme, Cynthia Fuller, Anne Bronte, Tupac Shakur, Williams Butler Yeats, D.H. Lawrence, Alan Moore, Alphonse Karr, and Dorothy Parker.

"On the Common Suffixes of Towns" | Some of the common suffixes of towns are —mere, -ton, -dale, -ville, -burg, and -wood. Thanks to the road trip that led to this information being sought.

Also by Kristi Maxwell:

Realm Sixty-four

Hush Sessions

Re-

That Our Eyes Be Rigged

PLAN/K

Bright and Hurtless

My My is printed in Adobe Caslon Pro.

www.saturnaliabooks.org